EMMANUEL JOSEPH

Masters of Innovation, How Tech and Real Estate Billionaires Drive Progress

Copyright © 2025 by Emmanuel Joseph

All rights reserved. No part of this publication may be reproduced, stored or transmitted in any form or by any means, electronic, mechanical, photocopying, recording, scanning, or otherwise without written permission from the publisher. It is illegal to copy this book, post it to a website, or distribute it by any other means without permission.

First edition

This book was professionally typeset on Reedsy.
Find out more at reedsy.com

Contents

1	Chapter 1: The Visionaries Behind the Curtain	1
2	Chapter 2: Building Empires from the Ground Up	3
3	Chapter 3: The Synergy of Tech and Real Estate	5
4	Chapter 4: Disruptive Innovations and Market Shifts	7
5	Chapter 5: The Power of Strategic Partnerships	9
6	Chapter 6: Sustainable Development and Environmental...	11
7	Chapter 7: Technological Breakthroughs and their Real-World...	13
8	Chapter 8: The Future of Urbanization	15
9	Chapter 9: The Role of Philanthropy in Innovation	17
10	Chapter 10: The Impact of Leadership and Governance	19
11	Chapter 11: Global Influence and Market Expansion	21
12	Chapter 12: The Legacy of Innovation and Progress	23

1

Chapter 1: The Visionaries Behind the Curtain

In the intricate world of innovation, the line between technology and real estate is often blurred by the visionaries who harness both sectors. These masterminds possess an uncanny ability to see possibilities where others see limitations. Their relentless pursuit of progress has created a legacy of transformation, reshaping the urban landscape and our way of life. From smart cities to the digital economy, these leaders are the architects of the future, designing solutions that challenge the status quo and set new standards for excellence.

These visionaries often start as disruptors, unafraid to challenge established norms. They leverage cutting-edge technologies to create breakthroughs that redefine industries. Their impact is not confined to their own enterprises; it ripples through economies, influences policies, and inspires a generation of entrepreneurs. As we delve into their stories, we uncover the common threads of resilience, creativity, and an unyielding belief in the power of innovation.

The journey of these leaders is marked by a series of calculated risks and bold decisions. They navigate through failures and setbacks with a tenacity that fuels their success. Their ability to pivot in response to challenges demonstrates a profound understanding of market dynamics and human behavior. This adaptability is a hallmark of their leadership, driving them to continuously evolve and stay ahead of the curve.

At the core of their success is a commitment to creating value. Whether through sustainable development or technological advancements, these leaders prioritize long-term impact over short-term gains. Their projects are characterized by a blend of functionality and aesthetics, catering to the needs of a diverse and ever-changing population. This holistic approach to innovation ensures that their contributions remain relevant and beneficial for generations to come.

As we explore the lives and achievements of these extraordinary individuals, we gain insights into the principles that guide their actions. Their stories are a testament to the transformative power of vision and innovation. By understanding their strategies and philosophies, we can draw inspiration to drive our own pursuits of progress and excellence.

2

Chapter 2: Building Empires from the Ground Up

The foundation of every successful venture lies in its inception. For tech and real estate billionaires, the journey begins with a clear vision and an unwavering dedication to turning that vision into reality. These leaders are not only builders of businesses but also architects of empires. Their ability to identify opportunities and act decisively sets them apart from their peers.

The process of building an empire involves meticulous planning and execution. It requires a deep understanding of market trends, consumer behavior, and technological advancements. These leaders are adept at leveraging data and insights to make informed decisions that drive growth and innovation. Their strategic approach ensures that every move is calculated and every investment is purposeful.

A critical aspect of their success is the ability to assemble and lead high-performing teams. These leaders understand the importance of collaboration and foster a culture of innovation within their organizations. They empower their teams to think creatively, take risks, and challenge conventional wisdom. This collaborative spirit is instrumental in driving breakthrough innovations and achieving collective goals.

The journey to building an empire is fraught with challenges and obstacles.

These leaders navigate through economic downturns, regulatory hurdles, and competitive pressures with resilience and determination. Their ability to stay focused on their long-term vision, while adapting to changing circumstances, is a testament to their leadership prowess. They view setbacks as opportunities for growth and continuously seek ways to improve and evolve.

Ultimately, the legacy of these leaders is built on a foundation of integrity and ethical conduct. They prioritize sustainability and social responsibility, ensuring that their ventures contribute positively to society. Their commitment to making a meaningful impact extends beyond their businesses, as they engage in philanthropy and support initiatives that address pressing global issues. By building empires that stand the test of time, these leaders leave an indelible mark on the world.

3

Chapter 3: The Synergy of Tech and Real Estate

The intersection of technology and real estate represents a fertile ground for innovation. Tech billionaires and real estate moguls leverage their expertise to create smart cities, sustainable developments, and interconnected communities. This synergy is driven by a shared vision of enhancing the quality of life through intelligent design and cutting-edge solutions.

Smart cities are a prime example of this synergy in action. These urban developments integrate advanced technologies to create efficient, sustainable, and livable environments. From smart grids and automated transportation systems to green buildings and digital infrastructure, smart cities exemplify the potential of tech-real estate collaboration. These projects not only address current urban challenges but also anticipate future needs, ensuring long-term sustainability.

The role of technology in real estate extends beyond infrastructure. It encompasses the entire lifecycle of property development, from planning and design to construction and management. Technologies such as artificial intelligence, blockchain, and the Internet of Things (IoT) are revolutionizing the way properties are developed and managed. These innovations enhance operational efficiency, reduce costs, and improve the overall experience for residents and tenants.

Collaboration between tech and real estate leaders is key to unlocking the full potential of this synergy. By working together, they can pool resources, share knowledge, and drive forward ambitious projects that push the boundaries of what is possible. This collaborative approach fosters a culture of innovation, where ideas are freely exchanged, and solutions are co-created.

As we explore the impact of this synergy, we gain a deeper appreciation for the transformative power of collaboration. The integration of technology and real estate is not just about creating smart cities; it is about building a better future for all. By harnessing the strengths of both sectors, these leaders are paving the way for a new era of innovation and progress.

4

Chapter 4: Disruptive Innovations and Market Shifts

Innovation is the lifeblood of progress, and tech and real estate billionaires are at the forefront of driving disruptive change. Their ability to identify and capitalize on emerging trends sets them apart as pioneers of the new economy. From the rise of the sharing economy to the proliferation of digital platforms, these leaders are reshaping industries and redefining the rules of the game.

Disruptive innovations often emerge from the convergence of technology and market demand. These leaders are adept at recognizing unmet needs and developing solutions that address them. Their ventures challenge established business models, creating new markets and opportunities for growth. This disruptive approach is characterized by a willingness to experiment, fail, and iterate until the desired outcome is achieved.

The impact of disruptive innovations extends beyond individual companies; it reshapes entire industries. The rise of ride-sharing services, co-working spaces, and online marketplaces are just a few examples of how tech and real estate leaders are changing the way we live and work. These innovations not only provide convenience and efficiency but also create new economic opportunities and enhance the overall quality of life.

Market shifts driven by innovation are often accompanied by a period of adjustment and adaptation. Established players must navigate these changes by embracing new technologies and rethinking their strategies. Tech and real estate billionaires play a crucial role in guiding this transition, providing leadership and direction in an ever-evolving landscape. Their ability to anticipate market trends and respond proactively is key to sustaining their competitive advantage.

As we examine the impact of disruptive innovations, we gain insights into the dynamics of change and the factors that drive it. The stories of these leaders serve as a reminder that progress is not a linear journey; it is a series of leaps and bounds driven by bold ideas and relentless pursuit of excellence. By embracing disruption and fostering a culture of innovation, we can unlock new possibilities and drive meaningful change.

5

Chapter 5: The Power of Strategic Partnerships

The journey to innovation and progress is often marked by the formation of strategic partnerships. Tech and real estate billionaires understand the importance of collaboration and leverage their networks to create synergies that drive growth. These partnerships are built on a foundation of mutual trust, shared goals, and complementary strengths.

Strategic partnerships enable these leaders to pool resources, share knowledge, and access new markets. By aligning their efforts with like-minded organizations, they can amplify their impact and achieve collective success. These collaborations often result in the development of innovative solutions that address complex challenges and create value for all stakeholders involved.

The process of forming strategic partnerships involves careful planning and negotiation. These leaders are skilled at identifying potential partners and assessing the value they bring to the table. They prioritize relationships that are built on transparency, integrity, and a commitment to mutual success. This approach ensures that partnerships are sustainable and beneficial for all parties involved.

One of the key benefits of strategic partnerships is the ability to leverage diverse perspectives and expertise. By working with partners from different industries and backgrounds, these leaders can gain new insights and develop more holistic solutions. This diversity of thought is instrumental in driving innovation and achieving breakthrough results.

As we explore the role of strategic partnerships in driving progress, we gain a deeper understanding of the power of collaboration. The stories of these leaders highlight the importance of building strong relationships and working together towards common goals. By fostering a culture of partnership and collaboration, we can create a more innovative and prosperous future for all.

6

Chapter 6: Sustainable Development and Environmental Stewardship

Sustainability is a core principle that guides the actions of tech and real estate billionaires. These leaders recognize the importance of environmental stewardship and prioritize sustainable development in their ventures. Their commitment to creating a better future extends beyond economic success to include social and environmental impact.

Sustainable development involves designing and implementing projects that minimize environmental footprint and promote long-term resilience. These leaders leverage green technologies and innovative practices to create buildings and communities that are energy-efficient, resource-efficient, and environmentally friendly. Their projects set new standards for sustainability and serve as models for others to follow.

Environmental stewardship is not just about reducing negative impact; it is about creating positive change. These leaders engage in initiatives that restore and preserve natural ecosystems, promote biodiversity, and address climate change. Their efforts contribute to the overall well-being of the planet and create a legacy of responsible leadership.

The journey towards sustainability is marked by continuous improvement and innovation. These leaders are committed to staying ahead of the curve by adopting new technologies and practices that enhance sustainability. Their willingness to invest in research and development ensures that their ventures remain at the forefront of sustainable development.

Leadership in sustainability also involves advocating for policies and practices that promote environmental responsibility. These leaders use their influence to drive change at a broader level, engaging with governments, industry groups, and communities to advance sustainable development goals. Their advocacy efforts raise awareness about environmental issues and inspire others to take action.

As we delve into the stories of these leaders, we gain a deeper understanding of the principles that guide their commitment to sustainability. Their actions demonstrate that economic success and environmental stewardship are not mutually exclusive; they can be mutually reinforcing. By prioritizing sustainability, these leaders are shaping a better future for all.

7

Chapter 7: Technological Breakthroughs and their Real-World Applications

The relentless pursuit of innovation by tech and real estate billionaires often leads to groundbreaking technological advancements. These breakthroughs have far-reaching implications, transforming industries and improving lives. The application of these technologies in the real world is a testament to the visionary thinking and ingenuity of these leaders.

One of the most significant technological advancements in recent years is the development of artificial intelligence (AI). AI is revolutionizing various sectors, from healthcare and finance to transportation and real estate. Tech and real estate billionaires are at the forefront of AI adoption, leveraging its capabilities to enhance efficiency, accuracy, and decision-making processes. The integration of AI in real estate has led to the creation of smart buildings, optimized property management, and personalized experiences for residents.

Another notable breakthrough is the advent of blockchain technology. Blockchain offers a secure and transparent way to conduct transactions, making it ideal for the real estate sector. Tech billionaires are using blockchain to streamline property transactions, reduce fraud, and increase transparency. This technology is also being used to create decentralized platforms that empower individuals and communities, fostering greater trust and collaboration.

The rise of the Internet of Things (IoT) has also had a profound impact on the real estate industry. IoT enables the seamless connection of devices and systems, creating intelligent environments that enhance the quality of life. Real estate billionaires are leveraging IoT to develop smart homes and communities that offer convenience, security, and sustainability. These innovations are transforming the way we interact with our living spaces and the world around us.

The application of these technological breakthroughs is not limited to urban areas; they are also being used to address rural and underserved communities. Tech and real estate billionaires are developing solutions that bring connectivity, education, and healthcare to remote regions. Their efforts are bridging the digital divide and creating opportunities for all, regardless of geographic location.

As we explore the real-world applications of these technological advancements, we gain a deeper appreciation for their transformative potential. The stories of these leaders highlight the importance of innovation in driving progress and improving lives. By harnessing the power of technology, they are creating a better, more connected world.

8

Chapter 8: The Future of Urbanization

Urbanization is a defining trend of the 21st century, and tech and real estate billionaires are playing a pivotal role in shaping the future of our cities. Their visionary thinking and innovative approaches are addressing the challenges of urbanization and creating sustainable, livable environments for all.

The future of urbanization is characterized by the development of smart cities. These cities leverage advanced technologies to create efficient, sustainable, and resilient urban environments. Tech and real estate billionaires are at the forefront of this movement, leading the charge in designing and implementing smart city solutions. These solutions encompass a wide range of technologies, from smart grids and renewable energy systems to autonomous transportation and digital infrastructure.

One of the key challenges of urbanization is ensuring equitable access to resources and opportunities. These leaders are committed to creating inclusive cities that cater to the needs of diverse populations. Their projects prioritize affordable housing, accessible transportation, and community engagement, ensuring that all residents have the opportunity to thrive. This holistic approach to urban development fosters social cohesion and economic prosperity.

The integration of green spaces and sustainable design is another critical aspect of future urbanization. Tech and real estate billionaires are championing the creation of eco-friendly cities that promote health and well-being. Their projects incorporate green roofs, urban gardens, and sustainable building materials, reducing environmental impact and enhancing the quality of life for residents. These initiatives contribute to the overall resilience of cities, making them better equipped to withstand environmental challenges.

The future of urbanization also involves the use of data and analytics to inform decision-making. Tech and real estate billionaires are leveraging data to optimize urban planning and management, ensuring that cities operate efficiently and effectively. This data-driven approach enables cities to respond to changing needs and trends, creating dynamic and adaptable urban environments.

As we look to the future, the role of tech and real estate billionaires in urbanization becomes increasingly important. Their visionary thinking and innovative solutions are shaping the cities of tomorrow, creating environments that are sustainable, inclusive, and resilient. By embracing the principles of smart urbanization, we can build a better future for all.

9

Chapter 9: The Role of Philanthropy in Innovation

Philanthropy plays a significant role in the lives of tech and real estate billionaires, who use their wealth and influence to drive positive change. Their philanthropic efforts are not just about giving back; they are about creating lasting impact and addressing some of the world's most pressing challenges. Through strategic philanthropy, these leaders are advancing innovation and making a meaningful difference in society.

One of the key areas of focus for philanthropic efforts is education. Tech and real estate billionaires recognize the importance of education in driving progress and empowering individuals. They invest in initiatives that provide access to quality education, promote STEM (science, technology, engineering, and mathematics) learning, and support educational institutions. Their efforts are helping to bridge the education gap and create opportunities for future generations.

Healthcare is another critical area where philanthropy is making a significant impact. These leaders are funding research and development of new treatments and technologies, supporting healthcare infrastructure, and addressing public health challenges. Their contributions are advancing medical innovation and improving health outcomes for millions of people around the world.

Environmental conservation is also a key focus of philanthropic efforts. Tech and real estate billionaires are investing in initiatives that protect natural ecosystems, promote sustainability, and address climate change. Their efforts are helping to preserve biodiversity, reduce carbon emissions, and create a more sustainable future for all. Through their philanthropic work, these leaders are demonstrating a commitment to environmental stewardship and responsible leadership.

Philanthropy also plays a role in fostering innovation and entrepreneurship. These leaders support initiatives that provide funding, mentorship, and resources to startups and entrepreneurs. Their efforts are helping to create a thriving ecosystem of innovation, where new ideas can flourish and drive economic growth. By supporting the next generation of innovators, these leaders are ensuring that the spirit of innovation continues to thrive.

As we explore the role of philanthropy in innovation, we gain a deeper understanding of the impact of giving. The stories of these leaders highlight the importance of using wealth and influence for the greater good. Through their philanthropic efforts, they are creating a legacy of positive change and inspiring others to do the same.

10

Chapter 10: The Impact of Leadership and Governance

The success of tech and real estate billionaires is not solely attributed to their innovative ideas and technological prowess; it is also a result of effective leadership and governance. These leaders possess a unique blend of vision, strategic thinking, and ethical conduct that sets them apart as exemplary leaders. Their approach to leadership and governance is instrumental in driving progress and achieving long-term success.

Effective leadership involves setting a clear vision and inspiring others to work towards it. Tech and real estate billionaires are skilled at articulating their vision and rallying their teams around it. They foster a culture of innovation, where creativity and collaboration are encouraged, and where individuals are empowered to take risks and challenge the status quo. This visionary leadership is a driving force behind their success and the success of their ventures.

Strategic thinking is another critical aspect of effective leadership. These leaders are adept at analyzing market trends, identifying opportunities, and making informed decisions that drive growth and innovation. They prioritize long-term success over short-term gains, ensuring that their ventures are sustainable and resilient. Their strategic approach enables them to navigate through challenges and seize new opportunities, positioning them for continued success.

Ethical conduct is a cornerstone of effective leadership and governance. Tech and real estate billionaires are committed to operating with integrity and transparency. They prioritize ethical decision-making and hold themselves and their organizations to high standards of conduct. This commitment to ethics fosters trust and credibility, both within their organizations and with external stakeholders.

Good governance involves creating structures and processes that ensure accountability, transparency, and responsible decision-making. These leaders are skilled at establishing robust governance frameworks that promote ethical behavior, risk management, and compliance. Their approach to governance ensures that their ventures operate effectively and efficiently, and that they are aligned with their vision and values.

As we examine the impact of leadership and governance, we gain insights into the principles that guide the actions of tech and real estate billionaires. Their stories highlight the importance of visionary thinking, strategic decision-making, and ethical conduct in driving progress and achieving success. By embracing these principles, we can enhance our own leadership and governance practices and contribute to a better future.

11

Chapter 11: Global Influence and Market Expansion

Tech and real estate billionaires are not confined by geographic boundaries; their influence extends across the globe. Their ventures operate in multiple markets, and their impact is felt in diverse regions. Their ability to navigate the complexities of global markets and expand their reach is a testament to their strategic thinking and leadership capabilities.

Market expansion involves identifying and seizing opportunities in new and emerging markets. These leaders are skilled at assessing the potential of different regions and tailoring their strategies to suit local conditions. They leverage their expertise and resources to enter new markets, establish a presence, and drive growth. Their global expansion efforts create new economic opportunities and contribute to the overall development of the regions they operate in.

One of the key factors driving global influence is the ability to adapt to different cultural and regulatory environments. Tech and real estate billionaires are adept at understanding and respecting local customs, traditions, and laws. They build strong relationships with local stakeholders, including governments, businesses, and communities.

They adapt their strategies to meet the specific needs and preferences of each market, ensuring that their ventures are successful and sustainable.

Global influence also involves leveraging technology to reach a wider audience. These leaders use digital platforms and tools to expand their reach and connect with customers, partners, and stakeholders around the world. Their ability to harness the power of technology enables them to operate on a global scale and drive innovation across borders.

As we examine the global influence and market expansion efforts of tech and real estate billionaires, we gain insights into the strategies that drive their success. Their stories highlight the importance of adaptability, cultural sensitivity, and strategic thinking in navigating the complexities of global markets. By embracing these principles, we can enhance our own efforts to expand our reach and drive positive impact on a global scale.

12

Chapter 12: The Legacy of Innovation and Progress

The legacy of tech and real estate billionaires is defined by their unwavering commitment to innovation and progress. Their contributions have transformed industries, improved lives, and shaped the future. As we reflect on their achievements, we gain a deeper understanding of the principles that guide their actions and the impact of their work.

One of the key aspects of their legacy is the creation of sustainable, livable environments. Through their visionary thinking and innovative approaches, these leaders have redefined urban development and created cities that are efficient, resilient, and inclusive. Their projects serve as models for others to follow, inspiring a new generation of leaders to prioritize sustainability and social responsibility.

The impact of their work extends beyond the built environment to include advancements in technology, healthcare, education, and more. Their relentless pursuit of innovation has led to the development of groundbreaking solutions that address complex challenges and improve the quality of life for people around the world. Their contributions to these fields have set new standards for excellence and created a lasting legacy of progress.

Philanthropy is another key aspect of their legacy. These leaders use their wealth and influence to drive positive change and support initiatives that address pressing global issues. Their philanthropic efforts create a ripple effect, inspiring others to give back and make a meaningful impact. Through their generosity and commitment to social responsibility, they leave a lasting legacy of positive change.

Ultimately, the legacy of tech and real estate billionaires is defined by their vision, leadership, and commitment to making a difference. Their stories serve as a testament to the power of innovation and the importance of driving progress. As we reflect on their achievements, we are reminded of the potential we have to create a better future through our own efforts.

The journey of these leaders is a source of inspiration and a call to action. By embracing the principles of innovation, sustainability, and collaboration, we can drive meaningful change and create a legacy of progress. The stories of tech and real estate billionaires remind us that the future is ours to shape, and that through our collective efforts, we can build a better world for all.

Book Description

Masters of Innovation: How Tech and Real Estate Billionaires Drive Progress delves into the lives and legacies of visionary leaders at the intersection of technology and real estate. This book provides an in-depth exploration of how these trailblazers transform industries through disruptive innovations, strategic partnerships, and sustainable development.

The narrative unfolds the stories of tech and real estate billionaires who defy conventional norms, build empires from the ground up, and create smart, interconnected cities. Through their relentless pursuit of progress, they challenge the status quo, embrace risks, and continuously adapt to changing market dynamics.

Readers will gain insights into the principles that guide these leaders, from their commitment to ethical conduct and environmental stewardship to their strategic use of technological breakthroughs. The book also highlights their philanthropic efforts, which drive social impact and support the next generation of innovators.

Masters of Innovation not only showcases the transformative power of collaboration and visionary thinking but also serves as an inspirational guide

CHAPTER 12: THE LEGACY OF INNOVATION AND PROGRESS

for anyone seeking to drive meaningful change and leave a lasting legacy.

www.ingramcontent.com/pod-product-compliance
Lightning Source LLC
LaVergne TN
LVHW020743090526
838202LV00057BA/6212